MANAGING GREEN SPACES

CAREERS IN WILDERNESS AND WILDLIFE MANAGEMENT

By Suzy Gazlay

CRABTREE
Publishing Company
www.crabtreebooks.com

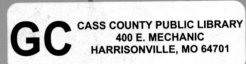

Crabtree Publishing Company

Author: Suzy Gazlay
Publishing plan research and development:
    Sean Charlebois, Reagan Miller
    Crabtree Publishing Company
Editors: Mark Sachner, Molly Aloian
Proofreader: Ellen Rodger
Editorial director: Kathy Middleton
Photo research: Ruth Owen
Designer: Westgrapix/Tammy West
Production coordinator: Margaret Amy Salter
Prepress technician: Margaret Amy Salter
Production: Kim Richardson
Curriculum adviser: Ruth Owen
Editorial consultant: James Marten, Ph.D.; Chair, Department
    of History, Marquette University, Milwaukee, Wisconsin

Written, developed, and produced by Water Buffalo Books

Photographs and reproductions
Alamy: Chris Fredriksson: page 9; FORGET Patrick: page 12 (center);
    FORGET Patrick: pages 12-13 (background); Jack Sullivan: page 15
    (bottom); Ron Niebrugge: page 16; GS International: page 18 (top);
    Gary Crabbe: page 18 (bottom); Ron Niebrugge: page 21 (bottom);
    David R. Frazier: page 26 (top); Maximilian Weinzierl: page 29
    (bottom); Nick Cobbing: page 38 (right); James L. Amos: page 40
    (left); David Keith Jones: page 51 (top); Arni Katz: page 52; Bob Gurr:
    page 54; Mark Conlin: page 58 (top)
Gary Carter Photos: page 5 (right)
Corbis: Sukree Sukplang: page 6 (left); Frans Lanting: page 6 (right);
    Phil Schermeister: page 23 (bottom); Jan Butchofsky-Houser: page 32
    (bottom); Frans Lanting: page 41
William Crawford, IODP/TAMU: page 45 (top)
Getty Images: Ethan Miller: page 35; Justin Sullivan: page 36
Bert Gildart: page 24 (left)
NOAA: page 17 (right)
Jennifer Olker: page 19; page 43
Parks Canada: page 19; page 23 (top)
Shutterstock: page 1 (top all); page 4 (all); page 5 (background); page 5
    (bottom left); page 7; page 8; page 11 (bottom); pages 20-21
    (background); page 25; page 26 (bottom); page 27; page 28 (all); page
    29 (background); page 30 (all); page 31; page 32 (top); page 33; page
    34 (top); page 37 (all); page 38 (left); pages 42-43 (background); page
    44; pages 46-47 (all); pages 48-49 (all); page 50; page 53; page 55 (all);
    page 56 (all); page 57 (all); page 58 (bottom)
Dr. Joseph F. Siebenaller, LSU: page 45 (center)
Sonoran Search and Rescue: page 34 (bottom)
The Elephant Sanctuary in Tennessee: page 51 (center); page 51 (bottom)
U.S. Fish & Wildlife Service: page 14 (left); pages 14-15 (background);
    page 17 (left)
USGS: page 39 (all); page 40 (right)
Debbie Waters: page 10
Wikipedia (public domain): page 11 (top); page 22; page 24 (right)

Library and Archives Canada Cataloguing in Publication

Available at Library and Archives Canada

Library of Congress Cataloging-in-Publication Data

Gazlay, Suzy.
 Managing green spaces : careers in wilderness and wildlife
management / Suzy Gazlay.
    p. cm. -- (Green-collar careers)
 Includes index.
 ISBN 978-0-7787-4866-3 (pbk. : alk. paper) -- ISBN 978-0-7787-4855-7
(reinforced library binding : alk. paper)
1. Wilderness areas--Management--Vocational guidance--Juvenile literature. 2. Natural areas--Management--Vocational guidance--Juvenile literature. 3. Wildlife management--Vocational guidance--Juvenile literature.
4. Outdoor recreation--Vocational guidance--Juvenile literature. I. Title.
II. Series.

QH75.G39 2010
333.78'2023--dc22
                                                                2009028145

Crabtree Publishing Company
www.crabtreebooks.com   1-800-387-7650

**Published
in Canada
Crabtree Publishing**
616 Welland Ave.
St. Catharines, Ontario
L2M 5V6

**Published in
the United States
Crabtree Publishing**
PMB16A
350 Fifth Ave., Suite 3308
New York, NY 10118

**Published in the
United Kingdom
Crabtree Publishing**
Maritime House
Basin Road North, Hove
BN41 1WR

**Published
in Australia
Crabtree Publishing**
386 Mt. Alexander Rd.
Ascot Vale (Melbourne)
VIC 3032

CONTENTS

WORKING IN THE WILD

Do you love being outdoors? If so, then you might dream of discovering a career that allows you to work outside. Do you have a special interest in animals? Does it bother you that some animals are endangered or threatened? Are you concerned about climate change and its impact on planet Earth? Have your friends and family noticed your love and enthusiasm for nature? If so, then your enthusiasm may have begun having an effect on your friends. Maybe you have already started helping the planet by sparking a concern in others!

Orangutans (near right) are losing their rainforest habitat in Southeast Asia. Stag beetles (far right) may not be as glamorous as the big primates, but they are also endangered due to the loss of old woodlands with rotting trees where the beetles can lay their eggs. Both of these species need protection and help. Would you enjoy a career protecting endangered animals?

A World of Wild Opportunities!

Perhaps you've had experience trying to help an injured animal or bird. Did you know that you could make this type of work your career?

Are you a hiker, a climber, a river rafter—or would you like to be? Can you imagine yourself leading others on adventures such as these, helping them enjoy and appreciate the wilderness you love?

Grasses and wildflowers are not what you would expect to see at the North Pole! Many species of wildflowers, herbs, grasses, mosses, and lichens grow on the Arctic tundra when the snow and ice melts during the summer.

Wildlife photographer Gary Carter (see Career Profile above) runs workshops for amateur and professional photographers (near left). Photographers come from all over the world to photograph in Gary's back yard.

Far left: Could you turn the leisure time outdoor activities you enjoy into your career?

WHAT IS WILDLIFE?

Mention "wildlife," and most people think of a bear or deer, or perhaps an eagle. Wildlife includes all living things that have not been domesticated (tamed or changed by humans). Earthworms and elephants, butterflies and snakes, eels and squid—these are all forms of wildlife. So are trees and wildflowers and algae—anything that's alive and natural. If you want to study wildlife, you'll be spending a lot of time outdoors or in the water—wherever the wildlife lives!

Maybe you're not so rugged and outdoorsy, but you like organizing and thinking up new ideas.

If any of these things sound like you, here is some very good news. Thousands of different jobs involve wilderness and wildlife! Some require being outdoors a lot. Some mix outdoor and indoor work. You could be the person who discovers new and important information about an animal, plant, or ecosystem. Your career could enable you to make a difference in the care, protection, and management of wild land and the plants and animals that live there.

Whatever your personality and your strengths, if you are interested in a career involving wilderness and wildlife, there are opportunities for you!

Marine biologists carry a sea turtle to a pen where she will lay her eggs at a hatchery in Phuket, Thailand. The scientists raise endangered sea turtles and then release them into the ocean.

Botanist (plant scientist) Hank Oppenheimer studies plants high on a boardwalk built over vegetation in Pu'u Kukui Watershed Preserve, Maui, Hawaii. The preserve is one of the wettest places on Earth and is home to animal and plant species that are found nowhere else on the planet.

What Is Wilderness?

When you think of "wilderness," what comes to mind? A remote backcountry high in the Rocky Mountains? Miles and miles of unbroken, snow-covered tundra in the northern reaches of Canada? Perhaps you're thinking of the vast expanse of the Sahara Desert, or the moors of North Yorkshire in the United Kingdom. It could be that you are imagining the dense rain forests of Brazil. Whatever image comes into your mind, it's likely to consist of a lot of land and be far from civilization, with little or no sign of human activity.

Wilderness is an area that has not been affected or changed by people and their activities. The only things that can change wilderness are forces of nature.

"A wilderness, in contrast with those areas where man and his own works dominate the landscape, is hereby recognized as an area where the earth and community of life are untrammeled by man, where man himself is a visitor who does not remain."

The Wilderness Act of 1964

Campers enjoy peace and breathtaking views in Utah's Redrock Wilderness. Conservationists have been fighting to stop oil and gas drilling in the area and the unauthorized use of off-road vehicles.

ENJOYING WILDERNESS

Official wilderness can't have roads or any types of structures. Motorized equipment and mechanical means of transportation are not allowed—so, no ATVs, snowmobiles, or skidoos! Horses, mules, cross-country skis, snowshoes, canoes, and kayaks are just fine—as are hiking boots. Wilderness areas are for use and enjoyment! Rather than the sounds and smells of civilization, visitors can enjoy clean air, the sounds of frogs and birds, and even the smell of freshly caught fish cooking over a campfire. Yes, fishing and hunting are permitted in many wilderness areas, as long as that area is not within a park or wildlife refuge—and, of course, only in keeping with fish and game regulations.

PROTECTING WILDERNESS IN THE UNITED STATES

In 1964, the U.S. Congress passed the Wilderness Act. Its purpose was to make sure that areas of wilderness would always be there for Americans. The Wilderness Act set up a National Wilderness Preservation System (NWPS) to protect wild lands in their natural state forever.

At the time the act was passed, scattered national forests were classified as "wilderness," "wild," or "canoe" areas. When the act was signed, areas of land in 51 different national forests became designated as wilderness. A total area of 9.1 million acres (3.7 million hectares) of land gained the protection of the NWPS. Since then, the amount of land protected by the Wilderness Act has steadily increased.

In March 2009, President Barack Obama signed a public land management act that designated 51 new wilderness areas. It created two million acres (809,371 ha) of wilderness lands—the largest expansion of public land in 15 years. As of March 2009, there were 704 wilderness preservation areas in the United States.

Each year, more than 3.5 million people visit Yosemite National Park to enjoy its waterfalls, granite cliffs, giant Sequoia trees (seen here), and areas of wilderness. Nearly 93 percent of the park's 761,266 acres (308,073 hectares) is wilderness.

Wilderness provides opportunities for solitude, recreation, or study that have no lasting effect on the land.

Most developed countries have some areas of public land that are owned and managed by the government. Some of this land is protected, and some of it can be used for different purposes such as recreation, logging, mining, or grazing. Some protected land is wilderness, but not all wilderness land around the world is protected to keep it from being used for something else.

Where Can We Find Wilderness?

Many areas of wilderness are within the boundaries of national parks, forests, and other government-owned lands. Yosemite's wilderness land sits comfortably alongside areas that include campgrounds,

picnic places, roads, and parking lots. There is a village with hotels, cabins, shops, restaurants, maintenance buildings, and gas stations. There is even a ski resort and a public swimming pool—all in the midst of beautiful scenery.

In terms of careers, parks such as Yosemite offer opportunities to work in beautiful surroundings either in the areas that are designated wilderness or in the many park businesses.

Green Spaces in a City

Urban parks are also known as public, city, or municipal parks. They come in all sizes, from tiny "pocket parks"—a place to sit outdoors—to large parks covering thousands of acres or hectometers.

Many urban parks have picnic areas and playgrounds. Some have sports facilities,

PROTECTING WILDERNESS IN CANADA

Canada is the second-largest country in the world with an area of about 3.9 million square miles (ten million square kilometers). Eighty-nine percent of this land is public land. That's nearly the same size as the entire United States! Much of this public land is not protected. Canada is home to one-third of the world's boreal forest (dense evergreen forest) and one-tenth of all forest cover in the world.

In November 2007, the Canadian government agreed to protect 25.5 million acres (10.3 million ha) of boreal forest. This was one of the largest wilderness agreements ever to be made in the world. Altogether, Canada's 42 national parks and reserves total 106,656 square miles (276,239 sq km) of protected land. This may seem like a lot, but less than eight percent of all of Canada's forested land is protected. About half of the rest—2.5 million acres—is open to logging. Nearly 90 percent of the logging is done through clear-cutting of frontier forests, a practice in which all trees are removed from a tract of land.

The Canadian boreal forest is one of the three largest "frontier" (unbroken, or uncultivated) forests remaining on Earth. The other two are in Russia and Brazil. The Canadian boreal forest is a prime source of timber and other resources, such as minerals and fossil fuels, that are key to the country's economy.

CAREER PROFILE

FREELANCE BIRD SPECIALIST: CONTRACT NATURALIST

My first taste of fieldwork was in college, where I did all sorts of surveys on animals such as birds, deer, and insects. Usually the surveys were done to locate animals in the wild. For example, we might want to find where certain raptor species (birds of prey, such as eagles or hawks) were nesting. It was physically demanding but very satisfying. It appealed to my love of the outdoors and wildlife.

Volunteering opened up a lot of doors for me. First I volunteered at a local environmental center and then at a research center. Because of these opportunities, I was able to make contacts in the research community. Later, I was able to find jobs through these contacts. Now, I do avian (bird) fieldwork for the state, park service, and universities. All my work has been either on contract (freelance) or as a volunteer.

In 2001, I began work as a seasonal naturalist during fall migration at the Hawk Ridge Nature Reserve. It was like being called home. I realized that this was my dream job—to work at such an amazing place with incredible people and tons of birds, and getting to share my passion for birds and nature with others. I've been there each fall ever since, both as an employee and a volunteer. As an employee, I develop and teach programs, work with the media, hire and train staff, and more.

I love the flexibility of my schedule and the variety of the work I do. Since I work out of my home office, I can take advantage of nice days to get outdoors and then do my office work in the evenings. You might find me giving a presentation to hundreds of people or standing in a remote field at 4:30 A.M., surveying birds.

Debbie Waters
Contract Naturalist, Hawk Ridge Bird Observatory
Duluth, Minnesota

trails, and even waterways and wild lands. These "green spaces" sit within town or city limits. They are usually staffed and managed by city government departments or government agencies that specialize in caring for a nation's parks and recreation areas.

Today, many people realize that parks can be more than just places of recreation. As gathering places for special events, youth activities, and more, they bring people together and build communities.

A young northern goshawk (pronounced "goss-hawk") at the Hawk Ridge Bird Observatory. Hawk Ridge is known for the large number of northern goshawks that migrate past the center each fall. The center calls itself the "Goshawk Hotspot."

Pocket parks are small urban parks that are open to the public. They are often created on a single vacant plot. In city centers, pocket parks are sometimes the only way to introduce some green space without an area undergoing major redevelopment.

"By building parks, a lot of communities are benefiting. For example, a park we built recently within 24 hours now stands as the play area for 4,000 children from that community. People can now walk, cycle, and play in that area, in an environment that is green and refreshing."

Luther Williamson,
Johannesburg City Parks,
South Africa

The Bedruthan Steps along the Cornish coastline in the UK is owned by the National Trust. Many UK residents are surprised to learn that the National Trust can buy and preserve beaches.

UK'S NATIONAL TRUST: FOR EVERYONE, FOREVER

In the UK, the National Trust is a charity completely separate from the government. It is supported entirely by donations and the money it raises. It is best known for buying and protecting more than 350 historic houses, buildings, and gardens.

The National Trust also looks after natural areas including forests, beaches, and nature reserves. As of 2009, it owned 710 miles (1,140 km) of UK coastline and was raising funds to buy more.

CAREER PROFILE

BURNING THE PRAIRIE: NATURAL RESOURCES PROGRAM MANAGER

My job is to oversee activities related to the natural resources, such as plants, animals, and the soil, at the Tallgrass Prairie Natural Preserve. One day I might be collecting surface water quality samples. The next I might be coordinating public bird and butterfly counts. It's all interesting, but burning on the preserve is always especially memorable.

Fire is natural and necessary to keep grasslands healthy and in balance. Tallgrass prairie once covered 140 million acres (56.6 million ha) of North America. Less than 4 percent remains, mostly in the Flint Hills region of Kansas where the preserve is located.

Fire would have occurred here naturally about every three or four years, but here, just like elsewhere in the world, fire has been suppressed. Trees always try to spread into an open area, so if the prairie goes too long without burning, trees will move in and take over. Therefore, we burn the prairie in a controlled way to recreate what nature would do. We burn separate parts of the prairie at different intervals.

CONTINUED ON PAGE 13 . . .

Kristen Hase
NRPM
Tallgrass Prairie National Preserve
Kansas

In 2008, for the first time in history, more than half of the world's population lived in cities. A United Nations (UN) report estimates that by the year 2030, 60 percent of the world's population (84 percent of people in more developed countries) will be urban dwellers. In the future, city parks where people can enjoy nature for a few hours or wilderness areas where people can vacation or spend day trips will become even more important.

Looking ahead

What does this mean for you and your future career? In this book, we'll be taking a closer look at some of the many prospects available to you. Keep in mind that many of these jobs will be within government agencies that oversee public land. Others will be with private agencies or universities.

Some careers will allow you to work independently, or freelance, marketing your own skills. If you want to work "green" in wildlife or wilderness, the possibilities are endless.

CAREER PROFILE

BURNING THE PRAIRIE: NATURAL RESOURCES PROGRAM MANAGER

. . . CONTINUED FROM PAGE 12

As a Fire Fighter Type II (the minimum qualification to be on a burn), I don't have a large role at an actual burn. My bigger responsibility is preparation. I determine the location of the burns each year and prepare burn lines to be mowed.

Usually a burn is done with two or three fire engines, several UTVs (utility vehicles) with water sprayers, and about 20 firefighters. Most of the time is spent preparing the back burn. This is a fire set to burn against the wind so that it goes slowly and is easier to control. After it has burned a wide area, the crew will go to the other side of the area to be burned and light a head fire. Head fires are wind driven and very intense. They move very quickly and would be nearly impossible to put out if the back burn area did not stop them.

After the burn, I record the burn areas and perimeters for future research.

Kristen Hase
NRPM
Tallgrass Prairie National Preserve
Kansas

A fire crew carries out a controlled burn (main photo). One member of the fire crew uses a special torch to ignite the grassland (inset).

WORKING IN PARKS, FORESTS, AND WILDERNESS AREAS

P ark employee – doesn't that sound like the ideal job for someone who wants to work outdoors? It certainly can be! Life as a park employee can include a lot of different tasks and experiences— many of them depending on where you work. Keep in mind: There are parks—and then there are parks!

Little and Large

On one hand, Pelican Island National Wildlife Refuge is a relatively small, five-acre (two-ha) piece of land off the Florida coast. Three employees take care of everything that needs to be done here—from keeping

The Pelican Island National Wildlife Refuge seen from the air (right), and one of the Brown Pelicans that live on the island (above). Brown Pelicans were once severely endangered in the United States due to poisoning from the pesticide DDT. Today, DDT is banned and pelican populations are on the rise.

an eye on the well-being of the birds, to interacting with visitors.

At the other end of the scale is Alaska's vast Wrangell-St. Elias National Park and Preserve. This huge area stretches across 13.2 million acres (5.3 million ha). This includes nearly 9.7 million acres (3.9 million ha) of wilderness. A large number of rangers work at this park. Their tasks include telling visitors about the historic "impossible" railway that was built

CAREER PROFILE

CONNECTING PEOPLE TO THE PARK: PARK RANGER

My role as a park ranger is to be a connection between park visitors and the park's wildlife and ecosystems. It is said that it is easier to care for something if you love it. We park rangers try to help visitors fall in love with our parks.

On a typical day, I open up the visitors' center and greet people, answer their questions, and tell them about the park. Later, I might lead a short hike around some of our trails. Every day on the park's trails we see wildlife such as alligators, wading birds, turtles, fish—the list goes on.

My greatest challenge is learning all there is to know about our park. It'll take a lifetime, and that still won't be enough.

My specialty? Some say I have an ability to always be at the right place at the right time and see the fascinating things out on our trails that others don't often get to see. I've seen alligators fighting and spotted some types of birds and snakes that usually stay out of sight.

Rudy Beotegui
Park Ranger
Everglades National Park
Homestead, Florida

A park ranger at the Everglades National Park holds a baby alligator while giving a talk to visitors about the park's wildlife.

"Our annual family vacations were in state and national parks. . . . I thought it was awesome that the rangers knew so much about plants, animals, history, and they got to live and work outside! Then in seventh grade I read a book entitled *Ranger In Skirts*. I loved that book so much I read it twice! Right then I knew no matter where I went or what I did in the future I was going to do something in or with nature."

Diane Barr
Teacher and seasonal park interpretive ranger
Juan Bautista de Anza National Historic Trail
San Juan Bautista, California

across the glaciers and other difficult terrain 100 years ago. The railway was built to connect two locations associated with a copper mine 196 miles (315 km) apart. The rangers also help hikers heading into areas so remote that they must be flown in and out.

A Career as a Park Ranger

Park rangers are undoubtedly the most familiar and visible employees of a state or national park. A ranger's job will involve different tasks depending on how large and busy the park is. In a small park, one ranger and a small staff may be responsible for everything. In contrast, in a larger, busy, popular park you may be one of as many as 50 permanent rangers and perhaps 25 or so seasonal rangers.

As a career park ranger you will typically start at an entry (lower) level and work your way up through the ranks. The level, or grade, at which newly hired park rangers start out

Park rangers carry out tasks such as issuing permits for hunting and fishing and giving visitors directions.

YOUR FUTURE EMPLOYER IN THE UNITED STATES?

The U.S. government owns about 30 percent of the 2.27 billion acres (1.1 billion ha) of land in the United States. This means that all this land belongs to U.S. citizens—and someone needs to manage it! This task falls to several different government agencies. If you want a career working with wildlife or caring for areas of wilderness in the United States, you might be working for one of these organizations:

• The National Park System (NPS) looks after all national parks, seashores, historic sites and monuments, plus recreation areas and preserves.

• The U.S. Fish and Wildlife Service (FWS) manages the National Wildlife Refuge System. This is a network of natural land and water areas. FWS conserves fish, wildlife, and plant populations and preserves habitats for endangered species. Many FWS sites offer hunting or fishing programs and are favorite locations for bird-watching and photography. FWS also produces a wide range of resource materials for environmental education.

• The Bureau of Land Management (BLM) oversees nearly one-eighth of the land in the United States, mostly in the West and Alaska. The BLM is responsible for balancing current use of the land with future need for renewable and nonrenewable resources. Among these are mineral resources, both above and below the ground. In this sense, the term "mineral" includes sand, dirt, gravel, and rock used for building, fossil fuels such as coal and oil, precious metals such as gold, and minerals such as phosphate.

• The Forest Service (FS) manages national forests and grasslands.

• The National Oceanic and Atmospheric Administration (NOAA) is responsible for national marine (saltwater) sanctuaries and estuary (river mouth, beach, and salt marsh) preserves.

Three special management systems contain lands from two or more of these agencies:

• The National Wilderness Preservation System protects wilderness areas.

• The National Wild and Scenic Rivers System cares for rivers, or sections of rivers, that have been selected for their beauty, wildlife, or recreation value. These rivers are allowed to run their natural courses without being dammed.

• The National Trails System is a network of scenic, historic, and recreational trails.

Working in wild habitats and with wildlife can take many forms.

Left: A U.S. Fish and Wildlife Service law enforcement agent shows illegal wildlife trade items, such as big cat skins, corals, and items made from the skins of endangered reptiles, that have been confiscated at U.S. ports.

Right: National Oceanic and Atmospheric Administration (NOAA) scientists on the "Hidden Ocean 2005 Expedition" strain mud collected from the seabed as they look for ocean creatures.

17

Park rangers are hard at work around the world. In Africa, rangers often spend most of their time dealing with the problem of poaching (the killing of endangered wild animals for food or to sell their body parts). Here, a ranger, or wildlife guard, protects African Savanna Elephants at a water hole in Mole National Park, Ghana.

depends upon their qualifications. Many rangers begin their careers as seasonal rangers, working only during the busiest time of the year.

In Canada and the United States, the top park ranger job is Park Superintendent. This person is an experienced ranger with exceptional management skills. He or she is responsible for planning and overseeing all the activities at the park. This includes visitor services, educational programs, safety, maintenance, planning for the future, and public relations. Superintendents may have worked at a variety of parks and had jobs at all different levels on their way to becoming superintendent.

What Does a Park Ranger Do?

Park rangers can be involved in many aspects of running a park. Interpretation work involves dealing directly with the visiting public. Rangers lead hikes and teach the local and natural history of the region.

A park ranger at Yosemite National Park leads a natural history discovery education walk for visitors to the park.

YOUR FUTURE EMPLOYER IN CANADA?

Parks Canada is the national park system for Canada. Parks Canada includes three different types of protected areas:

• National Parks are located in every province and territory. Each park represents a distinct natural area of Canada. They are protected and managed for the public to enjoy, understand, and appreciate, both now and in the future.

• National Historic Areas can be found in every province and territory. Each is important in its own way as part of Canada's history and culture.

• National Marine Conservation Areas (NMCA) divide Canada's oceans and Great Lakes into 29 distinct regions. NMCA is the newest part of Parks Canada. It reflects a significant feature of the country: the longest coastline in the world. Canada's coastline runs for 150,000 miles (243,000 km) along three oceans, plus another 5,900 miles (9,500 km) along the Great Lakes.

In 2009, more than 4,000 people worked for Parks Canada, including those at administrative offices and service centers. Rather than "rangers," the parks have interpreters who interact with the public and wardens who enforce the law.

Rangers in period costumes carry out a reenactment of Native American village life in an Iroquois longhouse at the Cartier-Brébeuf National Historic Site in Quebec, one of the National Historic Areas managed by Parks Canada. A single Iroquois longhouse was

CAREER PROFILE

CARING FOR AMERICA'S HERITAGE: NATIONAL PARK SUPERINTENDENT

I'm responsible for the management of my park, including programs and decisions that affect it. A typical day involves helping my staff with whatever they need to do their jobs.

What I like best about my job is that I get the opportunity to take care of a part of America's heritage—its national parks. I direct programs that bring back animals that have disappeared from the area, like the American bald eagles that were once permanent residents in the park. Because of intrusion by humans and the effects of chemicals such as DDT, by the mid-1950s there were no more nesting pairs. Between 2003 and 2006, we reintroduced 61 young bald eagles. Eight-week-old chicks were kept in a tower on one of the islands until they were about three months old and ready to fly.

In 2006, for the first time in over 50 years, there were not one but two successful nests. One has a webcam and can be watched live during nesting season. In 2006, people around the world watched as the first chick to hatch on the islands for more than half a century took its first flight.

CONTINUED ON PAGE 21 . . .

Russell E. Galipeau, Jr.
National Park Superintendent
Channel Islands National Park
Off the coast of Southern California

They plan and give presentations and answer a lot of questions!

Rangers in law enforcement head off problems among visitors, first by issuing cautions and warnings for violations of park rules and laws. If things get out of hand, they can enforce the law—they can even arrest someone! Rangers will sometimes investigate illegal activities in a park.

Park rangers take care of the safety of their visitors. They supervise campgrounds, enforce safety rules,

and sometimes chase off wildlife! They are also on hand to deal with medical or safety emergencies.

Park Rangers as Conservationists

One of the most important areas of ranger work is conservation. In fact, conservation is a top priority of national parks and preserves throughout the world. Conservation means taking care of natural resources and natural habitats and protecting them so that future

Below: A magnificent bald eagle in flight, and two one-month-old chicks in the nest. In 1967, bald eagles were officially declared endangered. The efforts of conservationists over the next 40 years resulted in their being removed from the Endangered Species List in 2007. The bald eagle is still protected, and it is illegal to possess a bald eagle, eagle parts, or eggs without a permit. Natives may possess bald eagle parts as they are an important emblem in many Native American cultures.

CAREER PROFILE

CARING FOR AMERICA'S HERITAGE: NATIONAL PARK SUPERINTENDENT

. . . CONTINUED FROM PAGE 20

I work with local communities and citizen groups to explain how and why park decisions are made. I'm particularly interested in showing people that we can save and enjoy these special places called national parks if we put our minds to it.

My greatest challenge is working with people who have very different points of view on an issue. For example, there are some who believe that species have always gone extinct so we shouldn't try to save them even if humans are the reason they are dying out. In the case of the bald eagles, some people thought that since they were already gone from the islands, why bring them back? Difference of opinion is healthy because it makes for a more informed decision.

Russell E. Galipeau, Jr.
National Park Superintendent
Channel Islands National Park
off the coast of southern California

"The greatest value [of my job] is that I get the opportunity to take care of a part of America and save it for enjoyment by future generations."

Russell Galipeau, Jr.
National Park Superintendent,
Channel Islands National Park,
off the coast of
southern California

generations will have them to enjoy. Conservation is also about using natural resources in a sustainable way. For example, if trees are cut down, they are renewable and can be replaced. If nonrenewable resources such as fossil fuels or minerals are used, these cannot be replaced. Therefore, they should be used sparingly without waste.

Park Rangers and Wilderness Preservation

Park rangers may also be involved in wilderness preservation. The difference between conservation and preservation is that conservation allows natural resources to be used wisely. Preservation means keeping the area exactly as it is and not using any of the resources. National forests and wilderness areas are both conserved. Wilderness areas are also preserved. No trees are cut in a wilderness; nothing is changed from its natural state.

As conservationists—and, at times, preservationists—rangers teach by word and example. They are the eyes and the ears of the park, doing what is necessary to keep it healthy for now and for the future.

Park rangers often join search and rescue operations to look for lost visitors. They also take part in rescues if a visitor is injured or gets into trouble.

Park Rangers as Specialists

Sometimes rangers may have specialist abilities or interests that they can use in their jobs. Some rangers serve as historians or

In parks with certain historic or cultural significance, a ranger may role-play an event as a way of teaching visitors history. For example, at Canada's Rocky Mountain House National Historic Site, costumed interpreters demonstrate skills, such as trap building, that would have been in use during the site's fur-trading days.

as archivists, recording, keeping, and organizing historical records.

A park ranger might be a naturalist or a geologist. As a naturalist, a ranger can help visitors who want to know more about the plants and animals in the area. A park's geologic features are

CAREER PROFILE

CARING FOR THE BACKCOUNTRY AND WILDERNESS: WILDERNESS AND TRAIL MANAGER

I'm responsible for managing the backcountry and wilderness program at the Shenandoah National Park. This includes more than 500 miles (805 km) of hiking and horse trails on more than 300 square miles (777 sq km) of land area. There are also 80,000 acres (32,375 ha) of wilderness.

I oversee backcountry recreation uses, such as day hiking, backcountry camping, climbing, horseback riding, and hang gliding. I check to see if they have any impact on natural conditions—for example, damage to trees or other vegetation. I'm also in charge of the preservation and maintenance of historic structures. We have seven backcountry Appalachian Trail huts and six cabins considered to be historic here in the park.

My responsibilities include supervision of backcountry staff and trails maintenance workers (more than 30 employees). I manage many hundreds of volunteers. Some conduct trail work, which includes erosion control and maintenance. Trail patrols hike the trails to check on campsite and trail conditions, as well as to provide information to visitors.

I like best the responsibilities and satisfaction that come with managing recreation use and visitor enjoyment. I also enjoy helping to protect natural and historic resources in the backcountry and wilderness of a major national park.

Steve Bair
Supervisory Biologist:
Backcountry, Wilderness and Trails Manager
Shenandoah National Park, Virginia

In some parks, rangers may be part of a mounted patrol. Here, a ranger greets visitors to the Crystal Forest in Arizona's Petrified Forest National Park. Being part of a mounted patrol would be the ideal career for someone who loves horseback riding and being outdoors.

BACKCOUNTRY RANGER

The ranger station in the Cutbank region of Glacier National Park is pretty rustic: a cabin and a barn built in 1917. Every summer, it serves as home and headquarters for the backcountry ranger stationed there.

Trails radiate out from the station in several different directions. The ranger's job is to patrol each of these areas, usually on horseback, and to "stay alert and expect the unexpected." A typical day's route may cover 20 miles (32 km) in eight to nine hours. Along the way, the ranger checks in with passing hikers, perhaps with a weather alert or wild animal sighting. In turn, the hikers may report a problem they've noticed. For example, if people are camping illegally, the ranger tickets them and sees that they move. If livestock from a neighboring ranch has broken through a boundary fence, the ranger heads over to the ranch to get help rounding up the animals.

a part of its unique environment too, often leaving visitors amazed at what lies beneath their feet or along the trail. As a geologist, a ranger can help visitors appreciate the land features and structures, as well as the effects of the forces that have acted on the land. Some rangers specialize in skills that can be used in particular parks. Snow rangers patrol their backcountry areas on skis. They are skilled in first aid in case they need to bring out someone who has been injured.

Become Part of the Park Team

Managing a park or wilderness area is very much a team effort with many career opportunities. Behind the scenes, ongoing maintenance is essential. Probably the most demanding is trail construction and repair—clearing brush

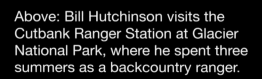

Above: Bill Hutchinson visits the Cutbank Ranger Station at Glacier National Park, where he spent three summers as a backcountry ranger.

Right: In this satellite image of Glacier National Park, we can see mountain ranges, green valleys, and glaciers.

and trees, digging out stumps and roots, scraping, leveling, building retaining walls and culverts—rugged work, but satisfying!

Park guides are seasonal employees. They collect fees, answer questions, and present programs such as visitor orientations. In these short talks, guides tell visitors about the history and special features of the park, let them know about upcoming programs or events, and advise them of safety issues and regulations. If you're thinking of a career with the park service, being a guide is a great place to start!

A popular summer job in many parks is working in guest services, which are known as concessions. These workers are the folks who staff the stores, restaurants, hotels, and other businesses in or near the park. Concessions work can be a great on-site experience, providing a glimpse of the inner workings of the park.

Concessions work might include waiting on tables, cooking, and cleaning. It might also include renting equipment, leading tours, driving buses, or assisting at meetings and conferences, depending upon the setting of the park. This work offers a great way to earn money, gain experience, and make new friends!

Protecting Forests

Trees and plants are essential for life on Earth. They make the oxygen we need to breathe, absorb the harmful greenhouse gas carbon dioxide from the air, and provide a habitat for millions of species of mammals, birds, and insects. Organizations around the world are working hard to protect and preserve forests.

In the United States, the U.S. Forest Service has the responsibility of managing the nation's forests and grasslands. Its mission is "sustaining the health, diversity, and productivity of the Nation's forests and grasslands to meet the needs of present and future generations."

Forest services employ workers to grow new stock to replenish the forests when wood is felled for lumber. Here, the nursery manager at the Lucky Peak Nursery, near Boise, Idaho, checks on englemann spruce seedlings growing in a greenhouse.

URBAN PARKLANDS

City parks are public lands, too. Some may not seem very wild. Still, these green spaces are places where people can be outside and interact with nature. They are an important part of community life, and there are often jobs connected with them. Urban parks offer job opportunities such as organizing and leading activities or events. There is also a lot of work to be done designing and building parks, and then maintaining them. There might be a good job opportunity right in your own neighborhood!

Forest Service Sampler

In the United States, there are more than 30,000 Forest Service employees working at hundreds of locations. Many of these employees begin their careers as volunteers. This gives them valuable experience and often increases their chances of being hired when a job opens up.

A forester's job has many variations. It might include measuring and grading trees, evaluating water samples or insect outbreaks, planting trees, laying out roads, fighting wildfires, and working with loggers.

Timber managers help plan and direct the harvesting of trees. They direct the replanting of the forests and market the lumber and products made from the forest's wood.

Fire experts deal with controlled burns, while forest service educators work with the public.

"History will judge the conservation leaders of our age, including our own leadership in the Forest Service, by how well we respond to these [environmental] challenges."

Abigail R. Kimbell,
U.S. Forest Service Chief

Forest technicians such as the one shown here report to timber managers. The technicians do much of the hands-on work involved in the felling of trees and processing of the wood.

CHAPTER 3

OUTDOOR ADVENTURE CAREERS

If you could go anywhere for a wilderness adventure, where would it be? What would you do? Maybe you're a high-energy person who'd like to scale a mountain or do some white-water river rafting. Maybe a slower pace sounds better to you, and you dream of a week or two of backpacking along the Chilkoot Trail winding through the Yukon in Canada or the Appalachian Trail stretching from Georgia to Maine in the United States. Or how about a wilderness trip where a mule takes the gear and you take the photographs? Here's something else to think about: What if you could make a living doing the very things you enjoy most? That's exactly what some adventurous people do!

Adventure holidays are big business these days. Canoeing, rock climbing, horseback riding, and exploring the rain forest canopy (all shown here) are all popular options. If you are outgoing, a good team leader, and outdoorsy with a big spirit for adventure, you might find yourself working in a career in which you get to give others the vacation of a lifetime!

Adventure for Fun and Profit

Many adventure-oriented careers are seasonal, so it's not unusual for people to have more than one job. How does this lifestyle sound: work as a river raft guide in the Grand Canyon in the summer, then teach skiing in Colorado in the winter? That's a pretty amazing way to earn a living!

High adventure careers can take you all over the world. Just about any type of expedition needs leaders and

CAREER PROFILE

CANOES ON THE RIVER: WILDERNESS ADVENTURE GUIDE

I own a company that offers guided canoeing adventures in the Canadian Shield and arctic wilderness of Manitoba and Nunavut Territory. I'm responsible for pretty much all aspects of running my company from marketing to organizing to taking care of all the details.

On the water I'm the guide, instructor, cook, and sometimes entertainer. I'm responsible for everyone's safety, and I'm the security guard as well if we are in polar bear or grizzly territory.

Before we start paddling, I'll explain to the people what our day is going to be like, how far we'll travel, and what sort of rapids we'll run into. Most of the time when we reach a rapid, we get out of the boats and "scout" it. This means I'll point out the route that we want to take to get through the rapid, and I'll point out any obstacles or areas that are unsafe. Usually I run the rapid first to show people exactly where I want them to go. Then I wait at the bottom of the rapid and play the safety guy, making sure that people are doing what they are supposed to do. If anyone tips over in the rapid, I get them safely to shore. Then I pick up the pieces that may have fallen out of their canoe.

Sitting around a campfire at the end of a day, it is so rewarding to see the guests realize that they have done something they have never done before. It makes my heart sing.

Rob Currie
Owner and Guide, Wilderness Spirit
Adventures Ltd.
Winnipeg, Manitoba, Canada

Dogsled safaris are a fantastic way to explore the wilderness of Canada, Finland, Norway, and Sweden. Guides teach visitors how to drive the sleds and care for the dogs. The guides then lead the groups of holidaymakers, each driving their own dogsled team, out into the wilderness.

WORLDWIDE WILDERNESS ADVENTURES—ENERGY, LEADERSHIP, AND FUN

Wilderness adventures take place all over the world and offer many ways to travel. Among the choices are canoes, kayaks, dogsleds, skis, snowshoes, horseback, rafts, hiking, and more. Opportunities for adventure travel are available to people of all ages, backgrounds, and abilities. Staff members are trained extensively in leadership, wilderness skills, and natural history. Teamwork is essential, and everyone works together to do whatever is needed. A high priority for staff members is enthusiasm and a commitment to serving the diverse people who participate in the adventures.

MOUNTAIN GUIDES— CLIMBING TO THE HEIGHTS

Mountaineering is a challenging sport on its own. Mountain guiding takes it to the next level, making for an exciting career. Experienced guides say that the reward is in the combination of the mountains, the people they work with, and confronting the challenges of the environment as they lead expeditions all over the world.

Guiding requires excellence in knowledge, skills, safety, and leadership. Another key ingredient is having a passion for the clients, the mountains, and the sport.

To be a mountain guide, a person must have mastered the sport, be in top physical condition, and have several years of climbing experience.

support staff. How about piloting a hot air balloon over the Serengeti plains of Africa as you answer your passengers' questions about the wildlife they see just below you? Or, perhaps you might guide people through the treetops of the Amazon rain forest, or lead a trail ride on the wild western side of Ireland.

Outfitters, Guided Trips, and Drop Camps

For many people, the perfect vacation is spending time away from civilization in the backcountry. Those who are independent and experienced can take off with a backpack of supplies and a trail map, but there are other ways to go about it. One is to have an outfitter provide everything that is needed for a trip into the backcountry. The adventurers can choose a "guided trip" in which the outfitter also supplies the guide and the agenda,

CAREER PROFILE

EXPLORING YELLOWSTONE'S WILDERNESS: OUTFITTER

I provide horse and mule adventure tours in the backcountry of Yellowstone National Park. Our pack trips are four, six, eight, and nine days in length, all out of doors. We do this as a family. Our three sons have gone on tours with us since they were very young.

A typical day in the backcountry begins at sunrise. Horses are checked in the meadow, and the campfire is lit for the cook to make coffee and breakfast. We greet the guests with a cup of coffee and give them the plan for the day's ride. After breakfast, the horses are saddled and lunch is packed. We are off on an adventure looking for wildlife. As we go, we talk to our guests about the terrain, geology (the history and structure of the rock formations around us), flowers, and other points of interest. Then we head back to camp for snacks and relaxing. Dinner is cooked over an open fire. We tell campfire stories, watch the sunset, and await the first stars of the evening. Then it's off to bed!

Mike Thompson
Wilderness Pack Trips
Yellowstone National Park
Emigrant, Montana

Left: Trail horses at Yellowstone National Park. Mike Thompson loves his work outfitting in Yellowstone National Park. Mike says, "Outfitting allows me to use my formal education in Animal and Range Science as well as my life experiences. My goal is to share my dream; keeping the traditions of western heritage alive and to provide visitors with the best possible backcountry experience I can."

NATURE EXPEDITIONS—FACE TO FACE WITH WILDLIFE

Do you dream about being within reach of a whale, sitting with mountain gorillas, walking among penguins in the Antarctic, or tracking tigers in India? Better still, how about being the naturalist who guides others through such unforgettable experiences? A wildlife tour guide needs to be knowledgeable about both the region and the different forms of wildlife. A guide must have leadership skills, get along well with people, be flexible, and enjoy teaching. This would be a wonderful career for someone who loves animals, people, and travel.

GALAPAGOS GUIDES— PROTECTING A FRAGILE ECOSYSTEM

Imagine working in one of the most biologically diverse areas in the world!

Galapagos National Park (Galapagos Islands off the coast of Ecuador) is a popular travel destination, but it is threatened by human impact. All visitors are required to travel with a certified naturalist guide, trained by the Charles Darwin Foundation and licensed by the park. Guides protect the park's natural resources by educating visitors and enforcing park rules and regulations.

In addition to leading regular tours, some guides lead special expeditions such as photography, birding, or diving. Guides are often among the first to spot a fire or eruption. They have even discovered some animals in areas where they were thought to be extinct.

Whale-watching boat trips give wildlife enthusiasts the chance to see the Earth's largest mammals up close and find out more about marine life with the help of an expert guide.

A tour guide introduces a tourist to one of the Galapagos Islands' endangered giant tortoises. Hatchling tortoises are often eaten by dogs and rats, so the tortoises' eggs are collected from the wild and incubated at the Charles Darwin Research Station. Once the young tortoises are large enough to resist predator attacks, they are released back into the wild.

or the outfitter may supply the equipment, while the adventurers choose a self-guided trip.

Another possibility is that people may want to hike into an area but don't want to haul all their gear. Then outfitters can do a "drop-camp." Using packhorses or mules, the outfitters deliver everything to the campsite. This is an especially good option for a film crew or research group with lots of equipment.

There are plenty of possibilities for building a career around helping other folks enjoy the wilderness.

Camps for All Purposes

Have you ever been to summer camp? Some camps are recreational, and some have a specific program— outdoor education, wilderness survival, or perhaps personal challenge such as Outward Bound.

Urban youth camps such as the City Kids Wilderness Project in Washington, D.C., and Snow-Camp in London take kids out of the city to experience a natural environment, often for the first time. Some camps are designed for people with special needs. Whatever the purpose, camps are a great way to work in the outdoors while making a difference in the lives of others.

Camp jobs vary depending upon the program, but just about every camp has counselors or group leaders, administrators, cooks and kitchen crew, maintenance staff, a nurse or EMT, a lifeguard, and program staff to lead sports and activities. Every job on a camp staff has the potential to have a direct impact upon the life of a young person.

Snow-Camp is a charity that gives disadvantaged young people from London's inner city the chance to try mountain sports such as skiing and snowboarding. Groups of young people get to spend a week trying winter sports in the French Alps. The camp includes a life skills course to help young people deal with issues they might face in their lives, such as drugs and crime.

SEARCH AND RESCUE

If a child wanders away from a campground and is lost, or a rockslide strands or injures a hiker, people trained in search and rescue are ready to help.

In many countries, the military includes search and rescue (SAR) operations. Some countries have agencies linking search and rescue with disaster preparation and response, and it may be that you'll find your ideal career there. Most often, however, SAR groups are nonprofit organizations of trained volunteers.

Among the volunteers may be SAR dogs and their handlers. An air-scenting SAR dog is trained to find the scent of a missing person and follow it, even when there is no other trail.

If you work out of doors, such as in a park, camp, or adventure job, SAR may be part of that job. In any case, as a person who knows and loves the outdoors, you might want to consider offering your skills and knowledge by volunteering with an SAR organization.

Dog and trainer teams excel at searching for lost people as well as victims of disasters who may be injured or trapped. Here, an SAR dog tries to pick up a scent in the desert.

This team, which includes highly trained volunteers and K-9 certified dogs, is ready to come to the aid of anyone who is lost, stranded, or injured in the Sonoran Desert region of the Southwest United States.

Ready for Emergencies—Wilderness Firefighters

Some of the most intense and demanding outdoor jobs take hours of training and practice in order to be ready at a moment's notice when lives may depend upon it. Some of the most challenging and rewarding jobs that involve saving lives and property are in wilderness firefighting.

Most firefighters in wilderness areas are seasonal workers, but they are trained and ready to go whenever and wherever they are called. Because of factors such as drought conditions resulting from climate change, the fire season in many wilderness regions is becoming longer than it used to be.

Typically, firefighter jobs are under the authority of certain government or regional agencies. In both Canada and the United States, an interagency organization serving multiple wild land agencies provides training and resources. In the event of a major wildfire, firefighters are brought in from all over as needed, some to fight the fire and some to back up areas left open when their firefighters have gone to the front lines.

Extreme Firefighting— Smokejumping

Not everyone would be willing to parachute out of an airplane into a forest fire, but that's exactly what highly trained smokejumpers do. Also known as parattack crews, smokejumpers are flown in to fight small fires in remote areas.

HOTSHOTS—THE BEST OF THE BEST

Hotshot crews consist of approximately 20 highly trained, well-disciplined firefighters. Their specialty is working at the hottest part of the largest, most serious wildfires, often in remote areas and without outside support.

Many countries, including the United States, Canada, and Russia, have hotshot crews ready to go wherever a major fire erupts. When they are not fighting fires, hotshots may be assigned to other jobs such as disaster response or search and rescue.

Hotshots have high standards, including physical fitness. When they aren't on the fire line, they spend at least an hour a day in physical training. This may include weight lifting, 5- to 10-mile (8- to 16-km) runs, or an hour or more of hiking uphill nonstop while carrying at least 60 pounds (27 kilograms) of gear.

Members of a California hotshot crew put out a fire in a mountainous desert area close to Las Vegas, Nevada.

SEARCH AND RESCUE IN THE CANADIAN AIR FORCE

SAR (Search and Rescue) Techs in the Canadian Forces are intensely trained specialists who carry out sometimes spectacular and often dangerous rescues in rugged and remote conditions. In addition to on-the-scene medical care and trauma life support, SAR Techs are skilled in parachuting, mountain climbing, SCUBA diving, and rescue techniques from a helicopter. They are experts in survival skills in all Canadian climate and weather and terrain (land) conditions.

SAR Techs have to be focused, tough, and in top physical condition. They are never done with training. When they are not out on a rescue or doing their weekly paramedic training, they are outside practicing their skills and working to stay in shape.

After they land, chainsaws and other firefighting tools are dropped in near them, along with food and water—everything they need to carry on for 48 hours. Once they land, their job is to quickly knock down the fire before it gets a chance to spread.

The United States and Canada have smokejumper crews, as do Russia, Mongolia, and other nations. Most crews are on 30 minutes' notice to be flown wherever they are needed. To be a smokejumper, you don't need previous parachute experience—you'll learn during training! You do need to be extremely fit and have at least a year's experience as a firefighter.

A trainee smokejumper wades from a lake after parachuting into the water as part of his training. Smokejumper training includes 15 jumps into different terrains, including open areas, forests, and lakes!

CHAPTER 4

OUT IN THE FIELD AND BACK TO THE LAB

W e can learn a great deal from observing the natural world. Still, there is much we don't know, and many questions to ask. Some of our questions come from curiosity: How do migrating animals know where to go, year after year? Some come from concern: What is causing Earth's climate to change? Some come from experience: What can we learn from the extinction of one animal species to keep it from happening to another? The way we find answers to these questions and more is through science research programs.

Why Go into Research?

Research scientists are on the front lines of discovery. It's exciting work! With today's rapidly advancing technology, researchers can learn and find answers beyond

If you like studying science and think you'd enjoy the challenge of solving problems through experimentation and by proving or disproving theories, then a career in scientific research could be for you.

> "I love what I do and really care about the research we do. All the research I have been involved with so far has focused on helping wildlife continue to thrive in spite of human changes to the landscape."
>
> Jennifer Olker,
> Junior Researcher,
> Natural Resources Research Institute at the University of Minnesota, Duluth

Research in the Field

A science lab isn't always four walls and a Bunsen burner. Research involving environments and living things means spending time out in the "field." Depending upon the topic, the "field" could be just about anywhere—from the ocean floor to a forest, or a river to an actual field!

Some field research can be done year-round, but much of it is seasonal, according to the natural cycles of the organisms and habitats.

Research isn't limited to one location, either. When Minnesota biologist Jennifer Olker looks at the relationship between amphibian communities and agriculture, her research takes her all across the upper Midwest, from Iowa to North Dakota—and she's not through yet.

USGS scientists fit a radio collar to a bobcat in a nature preserve in California. The scientists are studying the effects of road building on the bobcat's natural habitat and on its ability to move throughout its territory when the habitat is fragmented by human development.

A scientist tags a monarch butterfly as part of a research program to study the migratory patterns of the species.

ENDANGERED INDICATORS

Any endangered or threatened species is cause for serious concern. We hear of orangutans and sea turtles, giant pandas and spotted owls. Should we also be alarmed about smaller animals, such as frogs? Scientists say absolutely yes! Frogs are an example of indicator species—animals that are very sensitive to environmental conditions. They give early warning signals when an ecosystem is in trouble.

Right now, all over the world, many native frog populations are decreasing and even disappearing altogether. Something is very wrong. By monitoring frog populations, scientists can learn of potential problems that will eventually affect the other living things in the environment.

Frogs absorb water and air through their thin skins. Along with it, they take in even small amounts of pollution—acid rain, pesticides, and other chemicals. If the contamination doesn't kill them or make them sick, it can cause their offspring to be born with deformities. Another problem is increased ultraviolet (UV) radiation resulting from the decreasing ozone layer. Thin frog skin doesn't give much protection. Research suggests that UV exposure may interfere with egg development.

Other problems (stressors) threatening many frog populations include the following:

• Habitat loss as wetlands are drained and built over.

• Temperature change in air and/or water.

• Introduced species competing with the native population, overwhelming it and eventually replacing it. Sometimes the new frogs even eat the native frogs.

• Introduced non-native predators, such as large sports fish, that completely wipe out a frog population by eating eggs or adults.

• Disease spreading from fish hatcheries to the wild.

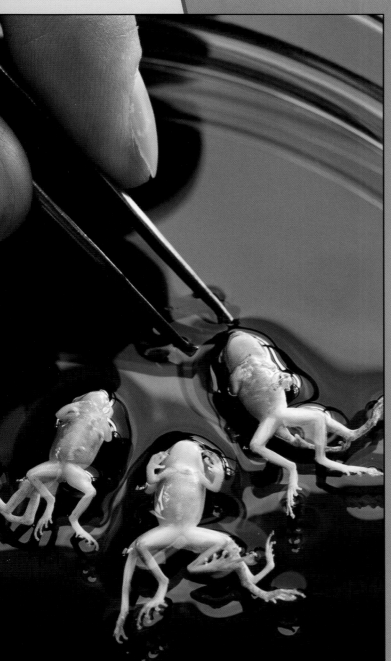

A scientist examines tree frogs that have developed with deformed hind legs. The frogs were found in a pond in Oregon. Scientists believe the deformities could be linked to water pollution caused by chemical fertilizers and pesticides.

RESEARCH ENVIRONMENTAL STRESSES ON FROGS: JUNIOR RESEARCHER

I'm the project manager for a project funded by the U.S. Environmental Protection Agency. We are studying the effects of different sources of stress on amphibian populations, including reduced water levels because of climate change, pollution, increasing water and air temperature, and more. Our research covers an area of the Northern Great Plains—Iowa, Minnesota, North Dakota, and South Dakota—that contains thousands of shallow wetlands. It's great frog country!

On a typical day during field season, I get out in the field around 9:00 or 10:00 A.M. Frogs sleep in and don't get moving until the Sun hits the wetlands. My crew and I put on our chest waders and search for frogs, frog eggs, and tadpoles. We also measure water quality, temperature, pH, and other indications of the quality of the habitat. We can usually do eight to ten surveys in a day.

CONTINUED ON PAGE 43 . . .

Jennifer Olker
Center for Water and the Environment/
Natural Resources Research Institute
University of Minnesota Duluth

Some projects take researchers all over the world. You might find yourself comparing the health of coral reefs in the Bahamas and Madagascar, or discovering previously unknown plant species in the rain forests of Ecuador. What kind of research would you like to do?

Life as a Researcher in the Field

It isn't at all unusual for researchers to carry equipment in a backpack and do the first part of their work right on the spot out in the field. There are samples to be collected, notes and photographs to be taken, surveys and measurements to be made, and data to be recorded.

A green frog, captured as part of a research program, is about to be weighed, measured, and examined for abnormalities. Frogspawn and tadpoles will also be collected for examination. A green frog will usually lay up to 7,000 eggs during the breeding season.

For scientific researcher Jennifer Olker, the chance to spend time wading around in wetlands looking for frogs is definitely one of the perks of the job!

RESEARCH ENVIRONMENTAL STRESSES ON FROGS: JUNIOR RESEARCHER

. . . CONTINUED FROM PAGE 42

After dark, we go out again to measure breeding activity by listening to frogs and toads calling to each other. Later in the summer, we catch as many young frogs as we can in order to weigh, measure, and examine them closely for malformations that might have been caused by UV radiation, pesticides, or some combination of stressors.

During the off-season, I spend most days working with the data we collected. I use many computer programs to create maps and write summaries describing the uses of the landscape surrounding our study wetlands, such as pasture or farming. My work involves extensive reading and constant writing. Data analysis is my specialty, but I also really like catching frogs!

Jennifer Olker
Center for Water and the Environment/
Natural Resources Research Institute
University of Minnesota Duluth

WHO'S ON A RESEARCH TEAM?

Every research team is made up of several people with different responsibilities.

The senior researcher is in charge. He or she develops the project's idea and obtains the funding. The senior researcher oversees the work and writes up the results into reports and publications. Senior researchers are highly experienced and usually have a PhD degree in their field of study.

The junior researcher is the project manager. This person oversees the details of the project, trains the technicians, and analyzes the data. Junior researchers usually have at least a Master's degree or several years of research experience.

A research team may also include any number of technicians. They carry out surveys, collect data, and process samples. Some are seasonal, working only during the field season. This is the time of year when they can observe the subject of the research in its natural setting. Some are hired year-round to continue to work with the samples and data.

Most people move up the research ladder step by step. Many researchers start out helping on a project as interns when they are first-year college students. Interns may not get paid, but interning is a good way to gain experience for the future.

Back in the main lab, samples collected in the field are processed to collect data. In a study involving wetlands, for example, this might mean picking insects out of clumps of wet, dead leaves and putting them into vials to be identified. Water samples might be tested for chemicals. Frogs might be dissected and their internal organs examined through a microscope to see how they have been affected by pesticides.

The Route of a Research Project

Most research is carried out through a university, a government agency, or a research institute. If you've ever done a science fair project, you've already carried out a research project on a small scale. You know that the first step is to decide upon a question to investigate.

CAREER PROFILE

A LAKE AT THE BOTTOM OF THE OCEAN!: GRADUATE STUDENT

Bill Gilhooly (above) on the research vessel and below preparing to make a research dive in the submersible.

I spent six weeks as a geochemist on the research vessel *JOIDES Resolution*. I worked in the ship's lab to help analyze and process samples brought up from the ocean's floor.

The voyage gave me a chance to study a subject important to my own research as a graduate student in the department of environmental sciences. Gas seeps are underwater springs that bubble methane gas, and sometimes oil, out of the seafloor. I wanted to learn more about how these seeps form. I also wanted to study the kind of carbon used by highly specialized seafloor animals that live near methane seeps. These organisms have a couple of food choices. They can eat methane that bubbles up through the seabed or carbon from dead algae raining down from the ocean surface.

This cruise gave me the chance to compare carbon food sources produced by photosynthesis (taking energy from sunlight) with those produced in the sediments using chemical energy. It also gave me the opportunity to work alongside accomplished scientists from around the world.

I have also made several dives in a submersible (a small research submarine). In the pitch black at the bottom of the sea, the sub's lights once picked up a colony of creatures few people have ever seen. They have adapted to living in the extreme, toxic conditions of a methane seep. On one very special dive, I went to a seep site called the Brine Pool. To see a lake on the bottom of the Gulf of Mexico was an incredible experience. I'd read many papers and seen many pictures of this seep, but nothing was better than seeing it with my own eyes.

Bill Gilhooly
Graduate Student
University of Virginia
Charlottesville, Virginia

CAREER PROFILE

STUDYING DESERT SOILS: SUPERVISORY BIOLOGIST

I'm the manager of a small research station for the United States Geological Survey (USGS). We study what happens to soil and plants when the soil is disturbed in arid (very dry) ecosystems around the world. My work takes place both in an office and in the field.

In the field, we typically go to remote sites and camp for at least ten days at a time. We work long hours making measurements and collecting samples. We sleep in tents, get pretty grubby, and experience a lot of beautiful places.

Our fieldwork takes us all over the world. I've worked in East Africa, Australia, central Mexico, South America, the Middle East, and around the U.S. Southwest. Our lab has projects in China and Mongolia, too.

CONTINUED ON PAGE 47 . . .

Sue Phillips
USGS Southwest Biological Science Center
Canyonlands Research Station
Moab, Utah

The next step is to find funding. This usually means applying for grants from public or private organizations that support research. For example, in the United States in 2009, the Environmental Protection Agency (a public agency) funded a five-year grant to establish Clean Air Research Centers that would research the health effects of air pollutants. In Canada, the WWF- (World Wildlife Fund-) Canada (private) established the Species at Risk Research Fund for Ontario. These funds will support research projects that directly assist in the recovery of species at risk of becoming endangered or extinct.

Once the funding is settled, it's time to gather a team, decide how to go about doing the project, train assistants as needed, and get started. All along the way there's research and more research.

A career in scientific research will mean spending time in the laboratory and at your computer keeping records and writing up reports. It will also mean time spent traveling to different locations to carry out field studies. The places you get to visit might be as varied as tropical rain forests, the polar ice caps, or, like research scientist Sue Phillips, the grasslands of Africa. In your travels you will sometimes have the chance to meet and work with local people from many different cultures, such as the Maasai farmers (far right) who assisted Sue.

It's important to know what others have discovered that relates to the investigation.

Some projects are short and seasonal. Others may go on for years. A lot of time is spent organizing, studying, and thinking about the data collected in the field. At the end of the project—or, sometimes, along the way—the senior researcher writes a report about what has been learned. Other scientists with expertise in the topic review the report. Then it is published and becomes a resource for other researchers.

CAREER PROFILE

STUDYING DESERT SOILS: SUPERVISORY BIOLOGIST

. . . CONTINUED FROM PAGE 46

I'll never forget being way out in the middle of the Maasai Mara in Kenya, hours from a town or a paved road. I was leading a crew of Maasai warriors we'd hired as field hands. We'd been out for over a week working hard together. One day as we ate lunch and watched the giraffes graze, we talked about how the Maasai knowledge of their local ecology compared to my Western perspective. We were amazed at how different, yet complementary, were our views.

The Maasai have long been a pastoral (herding) tribe. For generations, their ancestors moved their herds frequently to feed on new grass and relocated their villages every few years before the nearby resources were depleted. They believed that their careful land management was good for the environment and sustainable and maintained the balance of nature. Today, most Maasai would probably tell you that the way their forefathers did it was good for the land. Scientific data would seem to agree.

Sue Phillips
USGS Southwest Biological Science Center
Canyonlands Research Station
Moab, Utah

WORKING WITH WILDLIFE AND WILD HABITATS

Are you considering working with animal wildlife? If so, you'll find opportunities all over the world. You might want to work in a sanctuary, a preserve, or a rescue/ rehabilitation center. You could work in a zoo or wild animal park, perhaps one involved in a captive breeding program working to save a species from extinction. Perhaps you'll join a global organization fighting to save endangered animals in far corners of the world, or even in your own country. If management sounds good to you, you might even run a center, refuge, or wildlife organization. Some career choices such as wildlife veterinarian, wildlife biologist, or zoologist require specific training, but they will land you right where the animals are.

A bird rescued from an oil spill may be exhausted and dehydrated, as well as poisoned by the oil. It needs special cleaning and a period of care and observation before it can be released back into the wild.

WHY THE WORLD NEEDS WILDLIFE

Everything in the natural world is where it is for a reason. Each organism, large or small, has its own role, or niche, in the ecosystem where it lives. A niche is about all the organism's relationships with its environment, living and nonliving. As long as those relationships are working smoothly, the ecosystem will be healthy. We depend upon this health for our survival, as well as enjoyment.

Why are there so many similar yet different varieties of plants, birds, insects, and other animals? The reason is that biodiversity—the multitude of different types of plants and animals—is essential, too, and for a number of reasons. Biodiversity makes an ecosystem more productive. It gives greater protection against disease. It means more opportunities for discoveries, such as medicines, and a greater variety of edible plants. Also important: Biodiversity provides unique beauty and interest to our world.

". . . biologists estimate there are between 5 and 15 million species of plants, animals, and micro-organisms existing on Earth today, of which only about 1.5 million have been described and named. The estimated total includes around 300,000 plant species, between four and eight million insects, and about 50,000 vertebrate species (of which about 10,000 are birds and 4,000 are mammals) ... Today, about 23 percent (1,130 species) of mammals and 12 percent (1,194 species) of birds are considered as threatened. . . ."

World Wildlife Fund

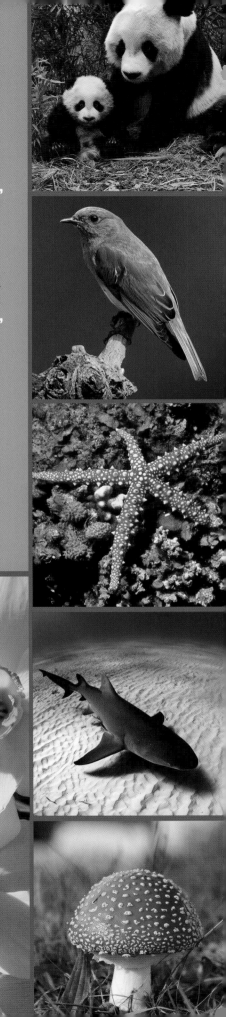

Saving Endangered Wild Animals

When it comes to saving endangered animals, working within an organization, where even the smallest steps add up, can give you a real sense of power, of being able to make a difference. Such organizations are becoming an increasingly loud voice calling the world's attention to the urgent plight of some of its wildlife treasures.

Save the Tiger Fund is one of many organizations focusing on a specific animal. Others, such as Canada's Pacific Wild organization, which is concerned with habitats and wildlife along Canada's Pacific Coast, target a certain region. Huge global organizations such as the World Wildlife Fund are committed to protecting life everywhere on Earth.

If your heart is with endangered species, you'll find opportunities all over the world, as well as close to home. The strength of wildlife organizations is in the commitment and diverse skills of the people who work there. They need administrators, office staff, media people; fundraisers, field workers, and educators. They need people with expertise in technology, finance, and legal issues, and so much more. Just imagine—your busy day in the office could make a difference to the lives of endangered tigers thousands of miles away.

What Causes Endangerment and Extinction

The number one factor causing the endangerment or extinction of plant and animal species is destruction of habitat, such as cutting forests, plowing open fields for pasture or farming, or clearing areas for development. Other significant causes include excessive use of plant or animal life: overgrazing, overfishing, overhunting, and overharvesting. Herbicides and pesticides, which take a toll beyond where they were applied, especially on aquatic animals, are also a factor.

Poaching—the killing of protected animals—can drive an endangered population into extinction. Increasing temperatures and changing water levels due to climate change add yet another stress. The photo below shows elephant ivory recovered from poachers being sorted by National Park Rangers at a national park in Kenya, Africa. Not shown: other body parts, such as feet removed from dead elephants to be used as furniture.

RESCUING ELEPHANTS

Hohenwald, Tennessee, is the home of a 2,700-acre (1,092-ha) sanctuary, but it's not for animals native to Tennessee, or even to North America. It's an elephant sanctuary, a refuge for both Asian and African elephants.

What are they doing in Tennessee? Since 1995, 24 elephants have come to live at Hohenwald. They are old and sometimes sick, retired from zoos and circuses. Under no circumstances do they perform or entertain visitors. They come to Hohenwald to live out their remaining days as elephants, roaming free with other elephants in a natural habitat.

Big animals need lots of space – more than most zoos can provide. One solution is elephant sanctuaries, such as the Hohenwald sanctuary in Tennessee. It's not their native Africa or Asia, but it's close enough for elephant friends Ronnie and Debbie, seen here (above). This group of student volunteers (right) spent their spring break cleaning and carrying out maintenance work at Hohenwald.

51

AVIAN HAVEN WILD BIRD REHABILITATION CENTER

Avian Haven, in central Maine, is a busy place, with a caseload of over one thousand birds every year. Along with emergency work, ongoing care, and preparing birds for release into the wild, workers respond to needs as they occur.

Diane Winn is the co-founder of Avian Haven. She says, "Like many rehabilitators, I got into this by being known as the person in the neighborhood who knew about birds. Neighbors began bringing me injured birds. I'd never heard of wildlife rehab. But asking around got me in touch with someone who dabbled in rehab. She shared her information with me. Once the door was opened, I was hooked on what very soon felt like my life's true calling."

Volunteers from the Chattahoochee Nature Center in Atlanta return a rescued baby great horned owl to its nesting area in a wooded suburban area.

Saving Wild Animals Closer to Home

Have you ever tried to help an injured animal or worked to save a baby bird that fell from its nest? If so, you know it isn't easy, and it doesn't always have a happy ending. Perhaps at the time, someone suggested calling a wildlife rehabilitator or animal rescue expert.

If so, that was good advice. Caring for injured animals, or raising young creatures separated from their mother, takes skill, knowledge, patience, and commitment. Wildlife rehabilitators are experienced in this work and have usually received some specialist training.

What Wildlife Rehabilitation Does

The purpose of wildlife rehabilitation is to treat and care for sick, injured, or orphaned wildlife. The goal is to be able to release them back to their natural habitat completely able to survive on their own, with their own species. Rehabbers

aren't wildlife veterinarians, although they often work closely together. It's more like being an emergency room doctor when an injured animal is brought in, and then a combined nurse, physical therapist, and caregiver until it is released.

Animal rehabilitation is challenging, and it's not a way to make much money. Most facilities are funded by grants and donations, and many rehabbers are volunteers. This work will put you in close contact with animals, however, and it can help acquaint you with what paid positions do exist at rehab centers, if you are interested in making this work your career.

CAREER PROFILE

RESCUING MARINE ANIMALS: MARINE MAMMAL CENTER MANAGER

My job includes caring for the seals, recruiting and training volunteers, and educating the public. We take professional programs to schools, meetings, or wherever we have an opportunity, and we set up displays at public events and festivals. Some days I go out to public beaches to do rescues. Other days are spent doing paperwork at the computer.

I started out as a volunteer caring for the seals. I loved it, especially working with the public. I have the best job in the world!

My primary responsibility is caring for seals and sea lions at our site. To do this, I schedule trained volunteers and keep the supplies they need on hand. We have a truck and rescue equipment, such as nets and herding boards, ready to go at any time. When an animal comes in, we start feeding and rehydrating immediately. The animals get a special fish-based formula until they are able to eat normally again.

One very exciting rescue was of a stranded adult Risso's dolphin weighing about 900 pounds (400 kg). We needed the help of a boom truck to lift the dolphin in its carrier off the beach so that we could back our truck under it! The media coverage of this and other rescues has helped publicize the mission of the organization.

Sue Andrews
The Marine Mammal Center
Manager, Monterey Bay Operations
Moss Landing, California

A team of experts captures an injured Harbor seal. The seal will be cared for at a seal rescue center and then released back into the wild.

BRINGING BACK THE ELK: WILDLIFE BIOLOGIST/ RESTORATION PROJECT LEADER

Elk used to roam wild in Tennessee. Then they were gone for more than 150 years until we began to restore them in 2000. I'm the coordinator of this restoration project. I've transported elk all the way from places such as Elk Island National Park in Alberta, Canada. Then, after they are released, I monitor them. Most of my work is done in a five-county "elk zone."

One of the things I enjoy most is monitoring the elk with radio telemetry equipment. Every elk has a collar with a radio transmitter attached to it, and each animal has a different frequency. I have a receiver and antenna so I can follow the signals and find where they are. I look for them from the ground, which means a lot of walking and driving. Sometimes I use an airplane. In the early summer, I look for calves to see how the population is growing.

Another favorite part of my job is working with landowners who are having problems with certain elk eating their crops or gardens, or doing other damage to their property. I can help with fencing or scaring the elk away. If necessary, I can use an immobilization dart to capture the elk and relocate it away from the problem.

It is very rewarding to a wildlife biologist to be able to restore a species back to a portion of its former range.

Steve Bennett
Tennessee Wildlife Resources Agency
Morristown, Tennessee

Careers in Restoration

"Restoration" simply means putting things back the way they should be. Restoration ecologists, biologists, and other specialists, along with supporting organizations, work to repair habitats, reintroduce and monitor missing species, and otherwise restore natural habitats to a healthy balance.

During the last century, more than half the wetlands (marshes, swamps, river floodplains) around the world have been destroyed. The most common reason is to provide drainage for farming. Often they are filled in to make room for development.

The impact has been devastating to the plants and animals that lived there, as well as to animals such as migratory birds that depended upon them. Depending on the

A female elk wears a collar linked to a satellite tracking system.

location of the problem, any number of groups, including nonprofit groups, community organizations, forest and park services, and others, are working to restore these valuable lands. It takes careful planning and sometimes engineering. In addition, native plants need to be grown, planted, and cared for until the area is self-maintaining again.

Restoring Wild Places Damaged by Disasters

Fires, floods, landslides, and other natural or unnatural disasters change the face of the landscape. In the aftermath, more damage can take place. For example, after a wildfire, there are no plants to hold the soil in place. A heavy rainstorm can wash away the soil and fill local streams with silt. To prevent this, foresters and volunteers turn out in force to replant trees.

MISSING LINKS

Every environment has a food web that is part of its natural balance. When competition, overhunting, disease, or loss of habitat causes a link in that web to disappear, it throws everything off balance. If the missing link species can be reintroduced, the balance can be restored.

Reintroduction can also prevent a species from becoming extinct. For example, the animals in a food web in a forested area might include mice, rabbits, foxes, owls, deer, and the top predator, wolves. As long as the food web is healthy, some animals will eat, some will be eaten, some vegetation will be consumed, and the population numbers will stay balanced. If one link—the wolves—is removed, everything else in the web will be affected.

The absence of the predator wolves means that the deer population will increase rapidly. With so many more deer eating the vegetation, there won't be enough for the mice and rabbits. With less food, the populations of mice and rabbits will decrease, so there will be less food for the owls and foxes. Meanwhile, the starving deer will strip the vegetation to the point of killing bushes and young trees. The food web is way out of balance all because of one missing link—the wolves.

A forest food web in the Canadian Wilderness. Each arrow in the web means ". . . gives food to. . . ."

Invasive Species—Unwelcome Intruders

An invasive species is a plant or animal living in a habitat where it doesn't belong. The problem is that sometimes the invader does too well in its new surroundings! In its original habitat, natural predators kept it under control. Without those controls, the invasive species keeps multiplying and competing with similar plants or animals in its new habitat. Eventually it may take over completely, driving out the native species.

One of the worst invasive animals is the zebra mussel. Young zebra mussels are tiny and swim free. They traveled from their native Russia in ballast water in ocean vessels. When the ships discharged their ballast, the baby mussels went too. As a result, they are now a serious problem in North America, the UK, and several countries in Europe. These freshwater shellfish attach in great masses to any hard surface. They clog water pipes, damage boats, and kill other animals by competing for food or attaching to them so they can't eat.

In 1876, the kudzu vine was introduced in the United States as potential cattle feed. Kudzu is

After the Yellowstone Park fires in 1988, the Arbor Day Foundation began working with the U.S. Forest Service to set up a tree-planting program. Since then, the program has helped plant nearly 13 million trees in national forests across the United States. Here, a volunteer gets to work with a box of pine saplings.

native to eastern Asia, where it's kept under control by occasional hard freezes. In the southern United States, where it's warm, nothing kills kudzu vine naturally. It kills other plants by choking them out and smothering them, growing over bushes, trees, or even buildings.

Removing an invasive animal and reintroducing the native can be challenging and will not always be possible. When a non-native plant invades a habitat, the only way to get rid of it without using herbicides is to tackle it one plant at a time.

Zebra mussels cluster on a branch in a lake at Charleston Lake Provincial Park, Ontario, Canada.

A kudzu vine can grow one foot (30 cm) a day and be as much as 100 feet (30 m) long. If you cut it, you have to burn the cuttings, or they'll sprout all over again! Here, an area of forest is completely smothered by kudzu vines.

ENDANGERED SPECIES—THE KIUNGA TURTLE PROJECT

The Lamu Archipelago off the coast of Kenya is an important nesting ground for three different species of sea turtles. The World Wildlife Fund (WWF) has been working with local communities to protect the turtles both at sea and on the beaches.

WWF and the Kenya Wildlife Service are running a successful conservation project in the Kiunga Marine National Reserve at Lamu. Selected sea turtles are fitted with satellite transmitters and tracked as they travel to feeding grounds and nesting sites.

Understanding their migratory patterns and identifying their nesting habitat is key to successful conservation.

Your Wild Future

If you have been inspired by this book to think about your future career, that's great! Perhaps you might now be considering a career as a scientific researcher or an animal rescuer. Maybe a few years from now you will be loving life as a wilderness ranger or mountain guide.

Whatever job you choose, remember this: We all need wild, green places where we can relax, have fun, and enjoy nature. The animals with which we share planet Earth need safe, clean, natural habitats in which to live out their lives and raise their young.

If you choose to join the millions of people who work in the wild, you will be helping protect our natural world for generations to come.

Above left: A marine scientist checks the satellite tracking equipment on the back of an endangered leatherback turtle.

Below: Hard work, stunning wild habitats, incredible wildlife—could this be you?

It's exciting to have plans and dreams for the future. It's also exciting to try new things. While you wait for school to be over, here are some fun projects to help you find out what you enjoy doing and to whet your appetite for your future career.

JOIN OR START A CONSERVATION CLUB

Whether at home or in school, you and your friends don't need to wait to make a difference! Kids around the world are starting up and carrying out green projects such as recycling, cleaning up polluted areas, restoration, protecting wetlands or a threatened species, pointing out problems and concerns, speaking up about policies, and more. It's a great way to get involved locally and make a difference in your own community.

VOLUNTEER

The people whose careers are profiled in this book agree: The best way to get into a wildlife or wilderness-related career is to volunteer! Many of these careers have seasonal jobs—typically summers and/or weekends—that are open to students. A person who is doing a great job as a volunteer improves his or her chances of being hired as a seasonal employee. A seasonal employee who is doing well has an edge when it comes to a full-time job and career. Another benefit is that as a volunteer, you'll get an insider's perspective, which can help you be sure this is the field for you.

BE SMART, BE SAFE!

Please get permission from the adult who cares for you before making trips to new places or volunteering in your free time. Always let him or her know where you are going and who you are meeting.

JOIN A CONSERVATION ORGANIZATION

Many environmental and wildlife conservation organizations around the world welcome students. Different organizations have different objectives. Some work on global issues. Others concentrate on a particular piece of land or a certain endangered species. Look for one that focuses on a cause that is especially important to you. By joining, you can support important work and gain valuable experience in ongoing conservation efforts. You may even find opportunities to participate in conservation fieldwork.

SPREAD THE WORD

Others around you may not be as interested in helping the environment or simply don't know all that much about it. Your knowledge and enthusiasm can be wonderfully contagious to your friends, classmates, and others in your community! It's important, of course, to be sure of your facts as well as your goals. It's not always easy to share information in such a way that those who hear you end up agreeing with you. So, it's never too soon to be developing and practicing good communication skills. These will be especially important if you choose a career that involves interaction with the public.

REDUCE THE THREAT OF INVASIVE SPECIES

Here's a place—your home—where you can make an important difference right now, both by word and example. Invasive species often get their start from someone's home! The pet goldfish or turtle released into a pond; the pretty ornamental plants that escape from the garden and sprout in a nearby field or woodlot; the interesting critters brought home from vacation in a jar and later set free—these are all common ways that invasive species become established where they don't belong. Many people simply don't realize that these species will compete with native plants and animals and may very well run the natives out of their natural habitat. In addition to helping people understand the problem, you can set an example by learning which plants are native, planting them around your house, and encouraging others to do likewise.

FIND ALTERNATIVES TO PESTICIDES

Search the Internet and ask organic growers for information about non-chemical alternatives to pesticides and herbicides. Get permission to try them out around your home or school. Let others know what you learn about controlling pests and weeds in ways that will not put chemical pollutants into the environment or pass them through the food web.

GLOSSARY

aquifer An underground layer of rock, sand, or gravel that contains water

avian Having to do with birds

ballast Heavy material, such as gravel or sand, kept in the lower part of a ship to help give it stability

biodiversity Biological diversity—the numbers of different species of living things

boreal forest A belt of mostly coniferous forest and lakes, rivers, and marshlands stretching across the northernmost parts of North America and Eurasia. Also known as taiga, it is characterized by long, severe winters and short summers

captive breeding A program in which endangered animals are bred and raised in captivity as naturally as possible with a goal of establishing a stable and healthy population. Some programs work to reintroduce captive-bred animals into the wild if possible

clear-cutting A method of harvesting all trees in an area at one time, destroying the habitat and leaving the land prone to erosion

concessions Commercial businesses, such as hotels, restaurants, or shops, run on government land for the purpose of providing services.

conservation Wise use, preservation, and, when possible, renewal of natural resources to ensure the best social, economical, and environmental benefits

conserve To use resources carefully and sparingly, avoiding waste; to protect from loss or harm

domesticate To train or adapt an animal or plant to live and be of use in a human environment

ecosystem A complete community of living organisms and their non-living surroundings

estuary A region where fresh water from a river meets and mixes with salt water from the sea; often in the form of an arm of the ocean extending inland

geochemist A scientist who studies the chemical composition of Earth and other celestial bodies

habitat loss The destruction of natural habitat, often for commercial purposes, to the point at which it can no longer support the species that live there; also known as habitat destruction

indicator species A species whose presence, absence, or health is evidence of the overall health of the habitat or ecosystem

invasive species Plants or animals that intrude upon a habitat or ecosystem where they do not belong, competing with the native plants or animals, and often overwhelming them; also known as exotics or aliens

methane seep An underwater spring that bubbles methane gas up through the seafloor

native An organism that originated in, and naturally belongs in, the habitat or ecosystem where it lives

niche The specific ecological role of a population of organisms within their habitat, including where they live, their position in the food web, and any influence they have on their environment

non-native An organism that lives in a habitat or ecosystem where it does not naturally belong

nonrenewable resources Natural resources that cannot be produced, regenerated, re-grown, or reused quickly enough to balance the rate at which they are being consumed

outfitter A person or organization that provides the supplies and equipment that someone else needs for an activity or some special purpose

preservation Complete protection of wildlife, ecosystem, or natural resource.

preserve To keep an area exactly as it is; to protect wildlife, wild lands, or natural resources totally

renewable resources Natural resources that can be replaced naturally at least as fast as they are consumed

research institute An establishment set up and awarded money for the purpose of doing research

stressors Physical, biological, or chemical conditions that can cause stress and affect the health of an organism or ecosystem

submersible A small underwater vessel used especially for deep-sea research

sustainable Capable of being continued or used with little or no long-term effect on the environment

urban Having to do with a city

watershed The land area that drains into a stream, river, or other body of water

FURTHER INFORMATION

www.goodworkcanada.ca/
www.planetfriendly.net/gw.php
Environmental jobs in Canada

www.pc.gc.ca/agen/empl/itm3-/emp3_e.asp
Parks Canada jobs

www.environmentalcareers.org.uk/careers/
Environmental jobs in the UK

www.nationalparks.gov.uk/lookingafter/jobs
Jobs with the UK National Park Authority.

www.environmentalcareer.com/
www.ecojobs.com/
Environmental jobs in the United States

www.nps.gov/personnel/
Park Service jobs in the United States

animals.about.com/cs/zoology/a/
aa081001a.htm
The Working Zoologist—overview of
wildlife-related careers (global)

www.nature.org/careers/
Wildlife careers with Nature
Conservancy (global)

usparks.about.com/cs/environmentalorgs/a/
conservationac.htm
Alphabetized list of international
environmental conservation
organizations, with links to the
Web site of each organization

usparks.about.com/cs/environmentalorgs/
a/blwildlifead.htm
Alphabetized list of international
wildlife protection and conservation
organizations, with links to the Web
site of each organization.

www.invasivespeciesinfo.gov/plants/
kudzu.shtml
An online video on kudzu, the vine
that ate the South

www.openroad.tv/video.php?vid=399
Watch the actual restoration of a
wetland after 50 years as a pasture

www.panda.org/wwf_news/multimedia/video/
Two Australians raise funds for wildlife
conservation projects. They then visit
the project to learn more about the
threatened species. (Six half-hour episodes,
each about a different threatened animal)

INDEX

INDEX

ABOUT THE AUTHOR

Suzy Gazlay is an award-winning teacher and writer of children's nonfiction books. Her experience includes developing educational curriculum, and she frequently serves as a content and curriculum consultant. She enjoys music, especially singing, and has written a collection of songs for children highlighting bits of science information. Suzy has always been fascinated by the natural world and loves to explore the coast or the Sierra Nevada Mountains near her home in California's Central Valley.

Printed in the USA—CG